DEATH VALLEY SCOTTY
BY
MABEL

Author: Bessie M. Johnson, 1932
Designed by: Alden Austin
Artist: Alden Austin
Coordinator: Esy Fields
Printed by Chalfant Press
Special thanks to: Sue Buchel and Michael Lawrence

INTRODUCTION

"Who was Mabel?" people will undoubtedly ask when they first see this little book, *Death Valley Scotty by Mabel*. Readers already know Death Valley Scotty, his well-publicized antics, "mysterious" gold mine, and "Castle" in the desert. They may even recognize the name of Albert Johnson, a wealthy Chicago businessman, Scotty's benefactor and true owner of "Scotty's Castle." But one person in this Death Valley adventure remains unknown, the small woman who quietly followed along with these two "desert rats." Mr. Johnson called her his wife, Bessie. Scotty called her "Mabel."

What did Bessie, a city woman, feel about being led into the desert? What did she really think about the flambouyant Scott who became her husband's friend? Many writers and tellers of this Death Valley tale have made suppositions, but few really knew the private Mrs. Johnson. Mrs. Johnson wrote her manuscript, *Death Valley Scotty by Mabel* to recount stories about the mysterious Scott. Her very personal accounts, however, also shed light on her private relationship with Scotty — and the desert known as Death Valley.

The description of her personal feelings about the desert may have significance in the broader context of Western American history. Scholars of 19th century Western history pour over women's letters and journals to learn their feelings about and impact on the settlement of the frontier. When their attention turns to the 20th century West, historians will look to documents such as "Mabel's," which contain personal accounts of the modern frontier experience. The value that Mrs. Johnson, a busy, urban woman, put on her desert treks may give scholars another example of the importance of the "frontier" in modern life. By understanding Mrs. Johnson's daily life, it may be easier to assess the significance of her experience as a 'Desert Mouse' traveling around with two big 'Desert Rats.'

A native of Walnut Creek, California, Bessie attended newly-opened Stanford University in Palo Alto, California for two years before transferring to New York's Cornell University. At Cornell she met Albert Johnson, a civil engineering student. The young couple married in Oakland, California in 1896 and resided near Albert's family in Oberlin, Ohio. From that point on, Bessie Johnson devoted her life to two things, Christian service and her husband, Albert.

Bessie almost lost her new husband in 1899 when a train accident seriously injured Albert and killed his father. Never fully recovering from his injuries, Albert nevertheless took over management of the family finances, and, with his father's partner, purchased the National Life Insurance Co. of Chicago, Illinois. The young Johnson moved to Chicago, where Albert became National's Treasurer.[1]

Devout Christians, Bessie and Albert joined the North Shore Congregational Church and became laity leaders for the next thirty years.[2] Their most important work, however, occurred outside their traditional church membership.

Mrs. Johnson experienced a religious conversion at a revival meeting in 1915 led by Paul Rader, later to become a worldwide evangelist. Mrs. Johnson introduced her spiritual mentor to her husband, and Albert soon joined his wife in supporting Mr. Rader's ministry. The Johnson's became bulwarks of Rader's evangelistic projects.[3]

Bessie Johnson used her previously untapped talent as a speaker to further Christian evangelism. Starting about 1925, she hosted a Rader radio program, "The Young Women's Council Hour," to meet the spiritual needs of young women. Bessie gave Bible lessons, answered listener's letters and gave both spiritual and practical advice to her young female audience.[4] She also made public appearances at Rader's revival meetings in Chicago and Los Angeles.[5]

Bessie Johnson continued her work with young women by becoming a leader in the Chicago Business Women's Alliance. The Alliance maintained an evening "lounging room" for single working women, provided affordable lunches, and offered supper each Monday night followed by a Bible class. At the Alliance's first annual dinner program, Mrs. Johnson introduced the guest speaker, Paul Rader.[6]

Bessie Johnson undoubtedly led an active life in Chicago as the wife of an influential businessman and as a religious leader in her own right. More and more, however, she found herself spending time in a location far removed from her city environment.

Her husband and the well-known Death Valley Scotty had become mining partners in the early 1900s, and this business relationship grew into a lasting friendship. Albert began to make lengthy annual treks into Death Valley with Scotty and his mules. After a few years, Bessie joined her husband on his vacations to the desert. She accompanied Albert and Scotty on camping trips and stayed in the rough accommodations at their Grapevine Canyon retreat.

As the Johnsons developed their Grapevine Canyon land into the fabulous Death Valley Ranch, popularly known as "Scottys Castle", Bessie continued her gospel work, conducting Sunday services for the workmen. She faithfully appeared as a speaker each Easter at the Death Valley Sand Dunes Sunrise Service. When the Civilian Conservation Corps opened a camp in Death Valley at Cow Creek, Mrs. Johnson carried her gospel to the enrollees each Sunday that she was in Death Valley.[7]

Word of Scotty's fabulous "Castle" had spread during the 1920s and curious Scotty fans drove long distances to see the new legend in the making. Not content with a view of the facades, the public increasingly asked to see the interior of the "Castle."[8] It became Mrs. Johnson's task to conduct informal tours for the public. By 1934, as many as thirty visitors a day would tour the Castle.[9]

Public interest continued to increase. Mrs. Johnson added staff to help give tours and by 1938, charged a fee to offset the added expenses. The staff also sold postcards of Scotty and "his" Castle. Visitation climbed to over 100 visitors on busy holidays.[10]

Mrs. Johnson wrote her "Mabel" manuscript in 1932, most likely while staying at the Castle, and contacted a few magazines to see if they were interested in a series of articles about Scotty. Her account may have been too personal for publishers, or she may have dropped the idea. At any rate the manuscript did not make an appearance in the 1930s.[11]

In response to growing visitor requests for Castle souvenirs, however, Mrs. Johnson completed a short book, *Death Valley Scotty's Castle, As Told by the Castle Guides.* The "Castle Publishing Co." had the book printed by the Progress-Bulletin, Pomona, California in September, 1941. The last page of the tour book advised readers to watch for a forthcoming companion publication, *Death Valley Scotty By Mabel.*[12]

Mr. Johnson obtained an estimate from the Progress-Bulletin for printing the "Mabel" book,[13] but the catastrophic events of December 1941 undoubtedly caused the Johnsons to "temporarily" shelve their second publication. Visitation to the Castle stopped abruptly as the country adjusted to its involvement in the World War. Mr. and Mrs. Johnson retained a few caretakers at the Castle, but rarely visited.[14]

By the end of World War II, Mrs. Johnson had passed away and Mr. Johnson was suffering from ill-health. He reinstated a staff to operate the Castle, but he seemed to have lost interest in publishing his late wife's manuscript. The legal-sized typed sheets remained, unpublished, in his file cabinet.

Only in 1986 did the manuscript come to light. The Gospel Foundation of California, keepers of Mr. Johnson's personal effects after his death in 1948, donated several file drawers of papers to the National Park Service's museum collection at Scottys Castle. Among those papers were two typewritten chapters of Bessie Johnson's manuscript.[15] The Death Valley Natural History Association, in publishing the "Mabel" manuscript, finally brings fifty year old source material to readers and scholars. That this material adds information to the Death Valley Scotty story goes without saying. Its hidden value lies in what it may tell historians about the importance of the West in 20th century American life.

Susan Buchel
Museum Curator, Scottys Castle
Death Valley National Monument

1. *Various sources, Scottys Castle Reference Library.*
2. *"Trustee Record, North Shore Congregational Church." A.M. Johnson Religious Affiliations, MSS 4, folder 1. Scottys Castle Reference Library, Death Valley National Monument.*
3. *Albert Johnson, letter to Bessie Johnson, 17 April 1916. A.M. Johnson Family Papers, MSS 2, Box 4, Folder 2. Larry Eskridge, "Only Believe: Paul Rader and the Chicago Gospel Tabernacle, 1922-1933," Master's Thesis, University of Maryland, 1985, p. 60.*
4. *Eskridge, p. 132.*
5. *Ruth Osterman interview at Scottys Castle, 1 Nov. 1985. Reference Card File, Scottys Castle Reference Library.*
6. *"First Annual Dinner Program," Business Women's Alliance, 28 Nov. 1921. Shadelands Ranch Historical Museum, Walnut Creek, CA.*
7. *Various interviews and photographs, Scottys Castle Reference Library.*
8. *Various letters, "Death Valley Ranch Papers," MSS 7. Scottys Castle Reference Library.*
9. *Linda Nelson Ewing interviews at Scottys Castle, March 1985 and 29 May 1985. Also AMJ letter to T.R. Goodwin, Superintendent, Death Valley National Monument, 13 Feb. 1941, MSS 19. Both at Scottys Castle Reference Library.*
10. *BMJ letters to AMJ, 17 Mar 1937 and 22 Mar 1938, MSS 19, Scottys Castle Reference Library.*
11. *Folder of correspondence "Death Valley Scotty by Mabel," MSS 19, Scottys Castle Reference Library.*
12. *Letter from Progress-Bulletin to AMJ, 21 Aug 1941, MSS 19, Scottys Castle Reference Library.*
13. *Ibid.*
14. *Various sources, Scottys Castle Reference Library.*
15. *Accession 1425, Death Valley National Monument Museum Records.*

Bessie Johnson

My name is not "Mabel", but that is what Scotty calls me, because he says I remind him of a girl by that name who used to ride a horse in the Wild West Show, and when she left the Arena the cowboys all said:

"There goes Mabel
Back to the Stable."

Scotty lives much in the days of Buffalo Bill's Wild West Show, in which he was a star cowboy for twelve seasons, and it is a little custom of his to call many of his lady acquaintances names of the performers in that fantastic show, as they linger in his memory.

For instance, a young aviatrix who comes occasionally to the Castle, he calls "Geisha," because her flying reminds him of a girl who used to do the high trapeze stunt. Another dignified woman he insists on calling "Freddie," because the particular shade of her hair matches a long lingering memory of Wild West days.

His passion for names, however, has not confined itself to reminiscences, for he has his own peculiar name for everyone. The girl at the Furnace Creek Inn, who talks for that establishment on the radio and who honored the Castle with her presence for dinner one day, is always known around the Castle as "Miss Radio." The girl at the curio shop goes very naturally by the name of "Curio." Al's (Al is my husband) old stenographer, who departed off this earth some years ago, and

1

who bore the name of "Miss Spurrier," is still known all over the desert as "Miss Sparrow," and if they can't remember "Sparrow" they call her "Miss Parrot," and everybody knows who is indicated. Victor Hugo's famous cafe in Los Angeles is dubbed "Berdugo's." Scotty often takes his friends to "Berdugo's."

Al and I

Al and I have traveled with Scotty all over the mountains and deserts of Southern California and Nevada for nearly thirty years. I suppose no woman knows Death Valley Scotty, his character and whims, better than I. I have traveled with him and suffered with him in all kinds of weather and under all kinds of conditions, from one hundred and thirty-five degrees in the shade to ten degrees above zero, in wind-storm and sand-storm, in balmy air that the Elysian Shores could not rival, and in whirlwind and cloudburst that seemed to rise out of Hell. You see when I got married, I got married for better or for worse, and I have had plenty of both; but, at that, it's been sweeter as the years go by. How could it be otherwise, for when I got married, it was for "better or for worse" - it didn't matter which. Now-a-days, many girls get married for "better" and when "worse" comes along they have a terrible time.

You know a man who travels the desert and loves it and lives in it is known in his own country as a "Desert Rat." I often say I am a little "Desert Mouse" traveling around with two big "Desert Rats."

There is such a thing as suffering a great deal of pleasure; at least I have suffered a great deal of interest and adventure, for neither Scotty nor Al come in duplicate. When I was married, a wee slip of a girl five feet high and weighing just ninety-five pounds, little did I imagine what I was stepping into. But somewhere in my ancestry there must have been a will to "play

Bessie Johnson - circa 1917

the game" at any hazard. Anyway, everything worth while in this world costs something and it has certainly been worth while to travel the sands of time with Death Valley Scotty and Al, down, down, into Death Valley, where the lizards run, the rattlesnakes crawl, the tarantulas jump and the scorpions and centipedes hide in the grey sage, down, down in Death Valley where the hot winds blow.

Scotty

Death Valley Scotty may live in Death Valley, but he's very much alive himself. He is of medium height, very stocky in build, with a large girth. He has a well-shaped head that sets well down into his broad shoulders. There are three things that impress you at once in his appearance, his alert grey-blue eyes, his clear fresh complexion, although he is close to sixty years of age, and his quick, firm walk. He walks like a soldier. He has a brain that works overtime and a philosophy all his own, for he has had no schooling but is widely experienced in the school of life. He spent his very early life as a small boy carrying water in buckets for miners and Borax teamsters in the desert that later became his beloved home. Here he learned through difficulty and hardship to think things out for himself rather than to rely on knowledge gathered from other people's experience and experiments.

I can see him now, as he lay back on the bench in the Castle patio the other night, smoking a cigar and looking up at the moonbeams playing through the grapevines hanging on the eucalyptus poles that crisscross the top of the patio. "Johnson," he said, "You want to change your tactics in making an attack; you don't have to step on a rattlesnake twice in the same place. If you step on his tail the first time, the next time step on his head. You got that?" And Scotty's eyes just snapped.

4

Scotty - circa 1900

5

There isn't anybody in the world who can talk just like Scotty. He has a phraseology that's purely Scotty phraseology and coupled with keen insight and a live wire brain, one forgets his rough manner and sits spellbound. I've seen Governors, Congressmen, Bankers, Lawyers, Doctors, College Presidents, Captains of Finance and so on ad infinitum, sit for hours with their mouths open around the table after dinner, while Scotty talked and figuratively speaking, just eat it up; anything that came into his mind, it mattered not what. He pulls his audience and the neighbors and the Castle and all his acquaintances to pieces and rips them up and down and back and forth, in no uncertain way, and Governors and College Presidents just sit spellbound. It's queer, that man! But you see, beneath it all, under the ten gallon hat which he always wears, beats a ten gallon heart and there's not a man in the desert who would do more for you if you were in trouble or jack you up worse and lambaste you more than Death Valley Scotty. He knows your weak points by instinct, but after all, he's fair and square, though he trusts no one.

In all our desert experiences, Scotty has never failed me. He is a wonderful cook, not by profession but by hard sense and oft-times necessity. One summer when quite a young man, he had to put in time between seasons in the Wild West Show in Paris. While there, he fell in with one of the leading preservers of fine fruits and this man taught him many things in the art of preserving. Each summer, to this day, Scotty puts in about a week preserving figs off our own trees at the Castle. These he gives away to his friends.

But he cooks for you as a favor only and indeed it is a favor. In the good old days before the Castle was built and we lived in a shack and two tents, My! The things Scotty turned off that camp stove! It makes your mouth water to think of them.

He always cooked a chicken apiece for the three of us and quail! Sakes alive! Hundreds of them all over the canyon and they get so tame and how Scotty can cook quail! With a strip of bacon, you know, a la Desert! And such cakes as he can make!

"Mabel, how'd ya like me to build ya a cake?" he will call.

"Sure, Scotty, go ahead. Build it high, a regular skyscraper with lots of floors to it." I reply.

A little later he may call: "The cake's all built, but I ain't got the overcoat on it yet. While I was about it I made some biscuit, but they ain't good, the skin got too hard."

And my! Such hot cakes as Scotty makes! You've never eaten hot cakes till you've eaten his. Just like feathers. Many's the time. after all the company's gone from the Castle, Al and I have gone down to Scotty's little hide-away camp, six miles down the canyon, where he escapes to when there are too many at the Castle. He just takes a run down there till "the fury quells," as he expresses it. And often, late in the evening, the three of us eat hot cakes and talk the situation over. You can eat a round dozen of Scotty's hot cakes and sleep like a baby after them, they are so dainty and delicious, with the finest maple syrup in the world and lots of butter. Scotty always buys the best.

The Castle

Everybody wonders about the Castle - why it is and what it is. That's what we wonder too. Scotty says it never had any beginning and it never will have an ending. And that's about true. It certainly is far from finished and it never really started. You see, we built a garage and storeroom first and two or three bedrooms overhead. We lived in this for a while and it was very ugly. Then we began decorating and glorifying it till it turned into a castle with an organ and a bell tower and chimes. Anyway, it makes a fine lodge when we come in off the desert,

Castle - circa 1948

8

hot and dusty. It's not nearly finished and maybe never will be. We don't know. We build as fancy leads.

During the main construction of the Castle, we had forty men at work and fifty Indians living in the Canyon and we had many guests. But Scotty decided last fall to close down the work for a while and close the Castle. So this winter, when guests came, as there was no cook or house help, except John, the little handy man of the place, Scotty and John and I all worked. Not long ago Al and I arrived on the place and found Scotty had a movie party of four on hand. The next day, as I had a couple of guests too, I took charge of the dinner. Just as we were ready to serve, Scotty came rushing into the kitchen and announced that a carload had just arrived, with an ex-governor and his party. I said "Scotty, that's fine, the more the merrier, but I am leaving the kitchen; I'll entertain the Governor in the reception hall and you take the kitchen." He said "That's all right Mabel, you handle the huey and I'll handle the pot."

Nobody can ever get anywhere with Scotty by being "Up Stage," as he calls it. He can always go them one better. The other day, coming through the desert, he met a man of so-called prominence and means who has a Dude Ranch near Beatty, Nevada. Scotty was in his little desert coupe, his pack tied on behind with ropes and covered with dust. He was hot and tired and worn after a long hard trip. The dude rancher, just driving in from his city home, was lounging on the back seat of a big, fine Duesenberg, with a driver in front, in uniform, etc.

They passed the time of day and finally the man said "Scotty, how do you like my car?"

"That car," said Scotty, "Why, that ain't no car. Is that all you got? My partner back in Chicago has Skeezers (Hispano Suiza's) in bunches like radishes."

A man by the name of Miller came to the Castle one day and, looking it over, said: "My brother has seven thousand acres of land."

"Is that all?" said Scotty. "We have seven million acres of land."

About that time a woman arrived with a bunch of tourists and, looking things over, with some scorn, she said: "I know a man who could buy this outfit and sell it."

"To hell with you," said Scotty. "We can buy this outfit and keep it."

But underneath all his roughness and bluster, how many times I have seen the hidden passions of tenderness and sympathy. All the animals on the place adore him. He hollers and yells at them and they just love it, that he should even notice them. The dogs love him so it's almost pathetic when he returns home after being away for a few days. They jump all over him and just bark and cry for joy. If he notices them they act like they want to turn inside out for sheer delight. Now, you know, there has to be something good in a man that dogs love. The mules love him, too, and rub against him when he pats them. And yet, how he hollers at them. It's funny about that man.

Only last night (it was the night after the election) I was sitting by the fire in the Living Hall alone, and Scotty came wandering in.

"Well," he said, "Roosevelt got elected, didn't he? Somehow I thought Hoover would get it. Johnson didn't, though. He said all along Roosevelt would get it. Johnson was right; but I guess it don't make much difference which one got it. They're both all right."

And then, as the fire burned brightly on the hearth, and the smoke curled lazily up the chimney, he settled back in the big leather chair, and began talking the world over in general.

"You know, Mabel, this world's in a pretty bad mess on the outside. Things is boiling all right." And he waved his hands rapidly in the air - a peculiar and very characteristic gesture he had. And then he went on:

"Now, there's Insull and Wingfield. They bit off more than they could chew. That's all that's the matter with them. I feel sorry for them."

"Yes, but Scotty," I said, "think of all the people who have lost their money."

"Yes," he said, "I feel sorry for them too. I feel sorry for them all. I tell you, Mabel, I ain't so dumb as they think I am. I ain't got none of them Boards of Directors and Trustees to tell me what I can do and what I can't do. You bet your life, I haven't. If I want to get on a mule and take a ride I just go, and there ain't no trustee to advise me about it. Now, you got that?"

At that, he went off to lie down on his bed and sleep the sleep that few men can sleep today - the sleep of the free man of the desert. And as I thought it over, I concluded Scotty was right; and I went to my own bed, happy and thankful to God for the path of the wilderness into which he had led me.

In the Mountains

But to really know Death Valley Scotty, you must travel with him on his mountain beats, with mules and packs. Many's the time we three have sat around the campfire in the twilight, the tired mules well hobbled and browsing about, the desert stretching out at our feet, its grey sage singed purple with the setting sun, and over our heads the glory of such a sunset as only God could paint' range upon range of great black moun-

11

tains rising in every direction round about; a beauty, a weird-ness, a charm, a desolation, a lure, a fascination, a loneliness, a delight, a "far-away-ness," a protectiveness, an in-dependence, a sense of possession and satisfaction that only the man with a desert instinct has the inspiration and capacity to enjoy and long for and cling to. It takes years to possess that instinct. It's a thing that grows inside of you. It's a thing that rises in a man triumphant over hardship and dust and temperatures and physical discomforts. It's the gift of Wilderness to the man who will brave its terrors and seek its lure. It makes or breaks men.

So, we sit around the fire in that place by itself, that place no other woman has ever been, and no other man but Scotty and Al, and Scotty begins to reminisce. China and Japan may tear at each other's throats, gangsters may shoot, Bolsheviks may rage, racketeers may send up the racket, Congress and the Senate may argue over the people's money, and the divorce courts may be busy, but way off in the desert, high up in a mountain, far from turmoil and graft and politics, and ban-ditry and depression, and wars and rumors of war, Scotty and Al and I sit around a water hole, as quiet and undisturbed as though we were on another planet. Fashions and changing styles and what other people think never disturb us there, for everything is ours, and no one is there to put a fence around it. We own it all - the desert, the mountains, the pinion trees, the mountain sheep, the sun and the stars. How rich we are!

I often think of a story my mother once told me. Two ar-tists were asked to paint a picture of their conception of perfect peace. One artist painted an exquisite little rural scene - a meadow, a brook, a flock of sheep, low hills in the distance. This represented his thought of perfect peace. The other artist had quite a different conception. He painted a great storm in the mountains, showing great black clouds with lightning flashing through them, and a wild, turbulent mountain stream dashing over mountain crags; but over the water stretched the bough of a tree; in a crotch in the bough was a little bird's nest; and in the nest were three young birds with the mother brooding over them. Storm all around but peace in the nest!

So, men may fight, and argue, and strive, and marry and trade in marriage, and buy, and sell; but way up in the crags in the wilderness, Scotty smokes his pipe of peace, and the white rays of the silver moon soften the great chasms round about, and the evening star glows like a blue-white diamond, and Orion and the Pleiades are all our own to enjoy. Our movies are the moving of the breezes through the pinion trees; our dances are the dances of the stars in their courses; and our stories are Scotty's romantic reminiscences of lingering memories.

Reminiscing

"You know, Johnson." I can hear Scotty say as he lies on his cot by the campfire and watches the smoke climb upward in fantastic figures, "when I went with Buffalo Bill's Wild West Show, we were showing in Europe, and we came to Monte Carlo. We showed about a month there, and every evening after the show the cowboys used to wander around the Casino to see what they might see. We weren't allowed to gamble, but we could look on. One night I saw a woman walking around there. She must a been about 35 years old, and I never saw so many diamonds on one woman in my life as she had on. Say, she had sparklers all over her. She must have had a hundred and fifty thousand dollars' worth of stones on her fingers and round her neck, and in her ears, and O, now I'm a-tellin' ya, she had diamonds on her! I just thought I'd like to meet that woman and find out how she got all them stones. So I walked up to her and tipped my hat and said 'Good evening, lady.' 'Good evening, cowboy,' she said. And so, we got to talking and finally I asked her; I said 'Lady, I never saw so many diamonds on any one woman in my life. I just wondered how you happened to get all them stones.' She looked at me and I'll never forget her answer as long as I live. 'Cowboy,' she said, 'I always go with the winner.' You know, Johnson, a winner never quits and a quitter never wins. Now, then, you got that?"

And Scotty went on soliloquizing:

"I was down in San Berdo the other day, and a man got me into one of them women's afternoon fandangos; you know, one of them afternoon affairs where they all talk and don't say nothing. And a "fly-up-the-creek" woman came up, all "a side-winding," and said: 'Now, Mr. Scott, I'm sure in your desert travels you must have lots of opportunities to do kind deeds. Won't you tell the ladies the kindest deed you ever did?"

"Well, lady," I says, "let me think a minute. One time several years ago I'd been traveling all day on a horse, and I came in on a dry camp way up in one of the canyons. There was an old road leading up to it; hadn't been used for years; but I noticed fresh tracks on it. When I got to the camp, there sat an old man and an old woman. They must have been seventy years old apiece. When they saw me they both began to cry, and I said: 'My goodness, how in hell did you two ever get up here?' Well, they said, they were driving through the Valley, and it was so hot they thought they were goin' to die, and they come to this road and they thought it led to a higher place where it wouldn't be so hot, so they took it and got up there, and it was night, so they camped there all night. In the morning they found their horse had wandered off. They had looked for him but he was gone, and they'd been there most a week and had no food. Well, I opened my pack and built a fire and made them a cup of coffee and fried some bacon and stirred up some saddle-blankets (hot cakes) for them, and say, you ought to see them two old folks eat! It cheered 'em up consider'ble. We sat around the fire all the evening and pow-wowed, and they was a nice old couple. We all slept that night on the ground. They was pretty cold, so I gave them a blanket I had. The next morning I made them some more coffee and gave them some breakfast. I had to be going, so I packed up and got astride my horse. I sort of hated to leave the old couple; they seemed kind enough sort of people; but there was nothing else to do; so I said good-bye, and they both was crying; said they'd sure die; no way for them to get out. They couldn't walk. It was a hundred miles from help, and there was no automobiles in those days. But I got on my horse and started off, and then I looked around and saw them two old people a-standing there crying, and, you know, I just couldn't stand it to leave them two old people there alone to die, so I just took out my rifle and shot them both. Lady, that was the kindest deed I ever did."

"Oh, Scotty," I said, "Why did you tell those women such a tale as that?"

"Well, you know all them bandits you meet when you go out; you got to tell them something, ain't you?"

"I suppose so, but it seems to me you might think up something better than that to tell at a ladies' club meeting."

"Well, that's what I told that bunch, anyway. You've got to send up some kind of a howl if you're going to be heard. There's so many free schools and so much ignorance."

And Scotty lighted another fifteen cent cigar (he always smokes the best), picked up his boots off the ground, turned them upside down, shook them, and then inserted a flashlight into each one methodically, as a matter of habit, to be sure no too intimate rattlesnake had made his bed in one of them, and, drawing them on, he threw a few sticks into the fire.

Rattlesnakes

Looking into his boots for snakes reminded him of one of the three times he had been bitten by a rattler.

" 'Bout the worst time I ever had with a rattlesnake was that time about twenty years ago. I was camping down in the lower end of Death Valley, and the mules got away. Well I spent a day tramping around the Valley and over them foothills looking for the mules. By night I was so tired I just threw myself down on a pile of brush and didn't pay much attention to what it was. Towards morning I woke up and felt something moving in my sleeve. I looked to see what it was, and there was the tail of a rattler sticking out from under my cuff. You see, he had crawled up my sleeve in the night to get warm. I grabbed his tail and pulled him out with a jerk, but I wasn't quite quick enough; he stung me right in the fleshy part of my arm above the elbow. I pulled my coat off and took my knife out and slashed the place where he had stung me, both ways like a cross, and let it bleed good. I didn't have nothing with me but some carbolic acid, and I poured a plenty of that in the wound and burned it. I usually have ammonia with me (that's better than the acid), but I didn't have any time."

"Well, I got out of that brush, and I seen it was a nest of rattlesnakes. It's a wonder I wasn't bit all over. As soon as I got the wound doped up I started to walk to Furnace Creek. It was a thirty mile walk, and, say, I thought it was 'curtains' for me. I was awful sick and had blind spells and everything. But I got there by night and went to bed. There wasn't anything to do but fight it out. I didn't eat nothing and laid there two days. A fellow was driving out to Goldfield on a wagon, 'bout a hundred miles, so I thought I better drive out with him and see a doctor. That was an awful drive. It took us three days, and I thought it was all over for me several times. But we finally got there and I went to see a doctor, but there wasn't anything he could do. He said the danger was over and I just needed to 'cuperate up a bit. But that was the worst time I ever had with a rattlesnake."

There are two kinds of rattlesnakes in the Death Valley country. On the higher levels in the mountains the snakes are large and long and thick; three feet long and over, and as large around as a man's wrist. They are more sluggish in movement than the smaller snakes, but more deadly, as their size gives them a larger sack of poison. On the lower levels, in the valleys, the snakes are smaller and are called "sidewinders" from their peculiar gait. Instead of the snakelike, serpentine motion of the big mountain rattlers, the sidewinders throw themselves from side to side. They look like they were coming towards you when they are going away from you. They run much smaller in size, averaging from eighteen to twenty-eight inches in length, and about as large as a man's thumb. They leave a trail on the sand of parallel cross bars, while the mountain rattlers leave a serpentine trail. Both species carry a sack of venom back of their jaws to which is attached a pair of hypodermic needles. When molested, they give the intruder a double hypo. But then, a rattlesnake is a very fair reptile, for he always give a warning to any who may encroach on his domain. He is most considerate if he has a chance, and every Desert Rat is familiar with that zz-zz-zz-zz and sits up and takes notice when he hears it.

Rattlesnakes are one of the hazards of the desert, though not as great a hazard as one might think. For they are only out and dangerous in hot weather. They hibernate in winter in holes in the ground and are very sluggish if found at all. In hot weather, when all humanity except real desert folks flee to cooler climes, the snakes are very lively and more or less dangerous to travelers. But, after all, there are not so many of them. You might live in the desert a year and never see one. Anyway, everything worthwhile in this world has its price. If you hunt elephants in Africa, you have to pay the price; if you would explore the North Pole, you must pay the price in cold and danger; if you would be rich in this world's goods, gain knowledge, or be an artist, each has its price. If you would travel the desert and ranges and roam the wastes of Death Valley, you must pay the price in danger and hardship, heat and cold, wind and storm. Scotty has never faltered or whimpered. He has paid the price the desert demands, and it's no small price. The danger in his case has been danger from reptiles, beasts, man and the elements.

Up in the high ranges are still found wild beasts - some bear, mountain lions, wildcats, and so on.

As we sat by the fire that night, I said: "Scotty, do you think any lions will disturb us tonight?"

"No," he said, "the mules will keep 'em off. I ain't never worried about lions when the mules is browsing around. One time I was way up in Tin Mountain and I killed a mountain sheep for meat. When I shot him he slid down a long slide about a hundred feet down. I wanted him pretty bad, so I got a rope out of the pack and fastened it around my waist and tied the other end to a tree and slid down to where he was. I dressed him, took all his insides out and skinned him and hung him up down there and climbed back up to where I'd left the mules, and I camped there that night. The next morning I went back to the slide, tied myself to the rope as I did before, and slid down. I wanted to get the meat. Well, sir, when I slid down to where I'd hung up that sheep, there were three big lions and they had ate every bit of that sheep up. When I landed there, two of them ran, but the other stood and looked right at me. Now, I'd done a thing I'd never done before; I'd left my gun up with the pack. Well, for a minute I thought I was done for. That brute looked at me for a second and then ran by me and grabbed me by the leg as he went and tore my trousers, and his teeth just scratched my skin. I climbed up that slide in a hurry, and that taught me a lesson. I'm never without my gun."

A Hidden Mine

For years Scotty has been supposed to have a hidden mine somewhere. Time and time again he has been trailed. Twice he has been shot at and wounded, and he carries a bullet in his body today as part of the price he has paid. Whether he has a mine or not, no man knows but himself. He still remains the man of mystery. Many have wondered where he got his money, and all kinds of wild stories have been told and written. Old settlers tell of by-gone days when he used to come out with sacks of rich ore. Some said it was ore he had gathered from samples in various collections that he had seen here and there, intimating that he had taken a piece from this and that place and put them together. Others thought he had really dug it out of the ground. But all this is just hearsay and rumor, for the fact remains that no man in the world has ever been able to fathom it.

It is true that he had has orgies of generosity, when he tipped bell boys $5.00 for carrying his grip up to his room, and paid newsboys $1.00 for a 3¢ paper. He has always been most lavish to me, in his own special way. When I am in Los Angeles, staying at a hotel, and Scotty comes to town, soon the delivery boys begin coming to my door with long boxes of flowers and big boxes of candy, till my room looks like a florist and confectionery shop combined, and it takes a good share of the hotel vases to care for the flowers. Flowers! All kinds! Short stems, long stems, orchids, violets and corsages by the dozen, to say nothing of gardenias, of which he is very fond. And candy! I couldn't eat even a small portion of it, there is so much. He has a special candy girl at a well-known confectioner's in Los Angeles, by the name of "Louise," who puts up all his candy just the way he likes it; for he is quite fastidious about it and he wants it just so. Louise is always kept busy when Scotty is in town. For he never sends me a five pound box of candy; he sends me two five-pound boxes, and, sometimes, on a special occasion, a twenty pound box. I often say to Al: "O, he sends too much." And Al says: "Let him do it, dear, if he wants to."

When Scotty does anything he does it big or he doesn't do it at all. He lives in a big country. His life is not hampered or cramped by formality or conventionality. What people may or may not think of him is something that never enters his head. His desert is big, his mountains are big, he looks out of his window across great spaces, his life is open and free and unfettered. Yet his personal wants are few and simple, and whether he sleeps in the castle or in the shack or on the ground in the mountains, it is all the same to Scotty. He sleeps quite as well one place as the other. But he does like to keep his body clean and is always bathing; and I have never seen Scotty in my life when he wasn't freshly shaven. Part of the water in his canteen is always kept to shave with. Many men who come to the desert feel it is a place where they can let their beards grow for a few days and rest their skin, and by the time they are ready to leave the desert they look like wild men; but not Scotty; he is as careful to shave when alone on the highest mountain as he would be among his friends in the city. He dresses the same way, summer and winter - a dark blue suit without a vest, a white shirt, a big tan sombrero hat, and a flaming red necktie. He is never seen in any other attire in town, and although often invited to the most ultra full-dress functions, he always attends

Al and Scotty - circa 1935

21

in his dark blue suit and red necktie. Nobody ever expects him to wear anything else. He wouldn't be Scotty. He says he can't be bothered with carrying around two or three kinds of clothes.

After a run of publicity, which he gets periodically in the papers, he always complains he had a terrible time with his red neckties. Women and souvenir collectors pull them right off his neck when he is walking down the street or in the hotel lobbies. So, he buys them in quantities and keeps several extra ones in his pocket in case of emergency. He told me confidentially not long ago that he had found a place where he could get them for fifty cents apiece, or five dollars a dozen. He said: "They're good enough for them bandits."

He is very friendly with all reporters and newspaper men, and all that I've ever met (and I've met a lot of them) seem to really like Scotty. And I must say, all the newspaper men who have been to the Castle have been most pleasant and gracious. As Scotty says: "They are human like everybody else; they got to make a living getting news; if you give them a square deal they'll treat you right." In fact, as I go about this world and meet and talk with thousands of people through my own walk in life, as well as through my association with Scotty, I have found that people are all pretty much alike, and that everybody has a heart hidden away somewhere. Scotty says some folks are more "stagey" than others, that's all. There's one woman sometimes comes to the Castle, whom he thinks is pretty stagey. She is very tall and carries her head high and is easily shocked at unconventionality. Scotty says she reminds him of the giraffes in the Wild West Show. They never would eat when the audience was looking. They held their heads high and looked around.

His experiences have made a he-man of Scotty, and to live and travel with him for twenty-eight years, as Al and I have, has only endeared him to us. We know his heart, and there is no one truer to his friends than Scotty. As he often says, "It's the easiest thing in the world to gyp and double-cross your friends, but it ain't to your credit."

Verbena

And so Scotty went on with his memories that night by the camp fire. "I saw Verbena the other day, Johnson," he said. "She was with a troupe of Indians, going up into Fish Lake Valley for the summer. Verbena was a right pretty Indian girl when she was sixteen. She must be about twenty-three or four now. I never will forget the time when she was living down in our canyon in the Indian camp, just about three hundred feet from the house. I was alone on the place, except for the Indians. Must a been about thirty of them in all in camp. Verbena was sixteen that summer and was due to have a baby. Well, one night Verbena began to holler, and I knew the time was ripe for the baby to arrive. I thought I'd go up to the camp and take a slant at things. I saw all the Indians around Verbena's tepee, standing and not doing anything excepting now and then one of them would moan and sing and holler in tune with Verbena. Well, I didn't see as there was anything for me to do, so I went home and went to bed. But after midnight, Verbena got to hollering louder and louder, and a lot of them Indians got to singing and yelling, and things grew worse and worse. You see, the baby didn't want to come. I couldn't sleep—things was in such turmoil around there. I thought I'd better not mix in, however, so I laid and smoked all night; and morning came and things wasn't no better. That baby just didn't want to get born, that's all. So, about six o'clock, a couple of Indian bucks went into Verbena's tepee to see if they couldn't help things along. One of them got on each side of Verbena and lifted her out of her blankets and put their arms under her shoulders and held her up and jumped her up and

23

24

down, to see if they couldn't help things along. Well, sakes alive! How she hollered! What she hollered before wasn't nothing to what she hollered when they was a jumpin' her. And all the squaws hollered, and O, I'm a tellin' ya, it was hell let loose. But the jumpin' didn't do no good. That baby just didn't want to get born, that's all. Things kept a gettin' worse till about noon, and then I couldn't stand all that ki-yi-ing down there any more, so I concluded it was time for me to take a hand. So, I got my biggest jack-knife out (the one you gave me, Johnson), and I washed it good in the dishpan, and I went down to the camp. I called Verbena's mother off to one side, and I told her: I said: 'Now, Dolly, you take this knife, and right on top of papoose's head is a soft spot, and you cut a little slit right in that spot, but be careful, don't cut too deep; don't cut into papoose's brain; then you get your finger under skull and pull papoose; if papoose dead, thro it away and bring me back my knife.' Dolly had a good deal of sense for an Indian, and she did just what I told her, and she pulled and the baby was born. Well Verbena, she stopped yelling right away. She said she was going to call the baby 'Daisy' because she liked flower names, and the baby was a girl. Nobody knows who the baby's father is. But Verbena loves Daisy, and every time I see them they are always together, and Verbena always pulls the hair apart on top of Daisy's head to show me the scar where Dolly cut her head so she could get born.

The Teamster

But the embers are burning low in the fire, and Scotty's tobacco is burning low in his pipe. He stretched himself and pulled his great watch out of his pocket.

"Well, Mabel," he said, "It's getting late—most nine o'clock. We better be going to bed. We got to get some sleep before the "Teamster" gets here."

25

"The Teamster!" O, if I only could describe it to you. "The Teamster" is Scotty's name for the morning star. He named it "The Teamster" many years ago, when he was a swamper for a driver on one of the twenty-mule-team borax wagons, as they crossed Death Valley. A swamper was a driver's assistant. He harnessed and unharnessed the teams and carried wood and water and was general handy boy. The teamsters always got up when this beautiful star appeared, and the teams were harnessed at early daylight, and they went on their way.

As we lay down on our cots that night, we were wooed to sleep by the rustle of the breezes through the cedar trees and the distant baying of a coyote and the occasional moving of our own hobbled mules. But it seemed we had scarcely closed our eyes when Scotty called out: "Time to get up, Johnson, 'The Teamster' is up." And we opened our eyes on the most beautiful thing God ever created for men to look upon.

There it came, straight over the Funeral Mountains, on the eastern side of Death Valley. That lustrous thing! The Bright and Morning Star!

You have never really seen stars till you have seen them in Death Valley. The clear, limpid atmosphere brings them very close. You feel you could reach up and pull them down. Ordinarily, a star looks about as big as a fifty cent piece as you look at it. But the beautiful Bright and Morning Star, as it comes up over the eastern horizon in the desert, looks as big as a large orange.

Most stars are golden in color. But the Morning Star in Death Valley becomes a shining white thing. Its rays and points are blue white, like a blue white diamond. It comes just ahead of the sun and heralds it. All the other stars fade out of sight, as it rises majestically towards the zenith, and for the space of a number of minutes it stands alone, supreme in the heavens, a glistening, scintillating gem. Then the sun comes gloriously forth, and the beautiful herald fades into its bosom.

I never see this marvelously majestic sight that my thoughts do not wander back to God's Holy Word, and I remember its promise of hope for this distraught, storm-tossed world, when the Son of God shall return back to this Valley of Death; first, as its beautiful Bright and Morning Star; and second, as the Sun of Righteousness.

And I am comforted.

For death loses it sting, and the grave its victory.

SECOND SKETCH

My first trip into the Desert will always remain a vivid, strange thing, in my memory. Al took me in, from Barstow, in the early days of automobiles. We left Barstow at two in the afternoon, and planned to camp, that night, fifty miles north, at a water hole, known as, "Granite Ridge," right at the foot of Pilot Knob, a tall outstanding table peak. About seven miles from Granite Ridge, he told me, we would go through Copper City, and he showed it to me on the map.

We had traveled along, through the sage, for three hours and had seen no one. Even today we often travel, on good roads, a hundred and fifty miles and never see a soul or pass a car. This is one of the charms of the Desert, after fighting your way through city traffic.

Finally, Al stopped and said: "We're here."

I said "Where?"

He said "Copper City."

"I don't see any city here, there's nothing here but a shack, a man and a mule. Does that make a city?"

He said: "Look over there and tell me what you see," and he pointed about fifty feet away.

"I see a stream of water, as big as your finger, coming out of a pipe."

And he replied, "That's what puts this place on the map.

Water! I had never realized its importance before. You must travel the Wilderness to know its value. The Desert can never be largely populated just for the want of water. This is the reason we will never have near neighbors at the Castle. Man cannot live without water.

We passed the time of day with the man and the mule, and then went on up to the Ridge to camp for the night, by another small stream of water. I shall never forget that sense of

Albert Johnson - circa 1917

weirdness, as the sun, hanging low in the west, cast long, dark shadows over the desert Ranges. The stranger to the desert has no conception of the vastness of this country. Canyon upon canyon, peak upon peak, range upon range; and as the long shadows enveloped the mountains, it looked more like Dante's Inferno than anything else to me.

This night at Granite Ridge was the first night I had over slept out-of-doors in the Desert. I was a sure-enough tender-foot and little did I sleep; although Al made me a fine bed and dug hip and shoulder holes, for me, in the sand. But O! How lonely and desolate it all seemed. About midnight I got out of the bed, he had put so much time on, and crawled into the car; it felt more like home.

How differently I feel now, after years of experience in the Desert. The peace of it is such a joy after the turmoil of life out side. The mountains are fortresses of protection. The canyons are full of interest. The long shadows, at night, are soothing. The sighing winds waft me away in beautiful dreams of unknown worlds, in the stars, that glitter and sparkle as I close my eyes and forget the restlessness of the world without.

Haunts

Scotty was bound for Granite Ridge several years ago. He had been across Death Valley and through Wingate Pass with the mules on his way to Barstow. About three miles from the Ridge he met a man and a woman with a buckboard and a couple of horses. Travelers in lonely parts of the Desert always stop and get acquainted if they meet anybody, for you might travel for days, in some parts, and never see a soul.

So Scotty stopped and said: "Hello, where you bound for?"

"We're going to Barstow," they said.

"Well you ain't agoin' there tonight," replied Scotty.

"Why not?"

"Too fur."

They looked troubled. So Scotty said: "You better come up there with me and camp tonight." And he pointed up to the Ridge.

"O," no," said the woman, "We ain't going to camp up there, we camped there last night and the place is haunted. We been traveling all day and lost our way. I guess we been going around in circles, because we left here, from this same spot, this morning for Barstow. But we aint going back up there; it's haunted."

"There's hants there, is there?" said Scotty.

"Yes, that place is haunted," said the woman emphatically.

"Well, what kind of hants are they?" asked Scotty.

"O," the woman said, "It sounded like someone was throwing stones at the rocks."

There are large boulders all around this camp.

"Well," said Scotty, "It's the only good place to get good water around here, and it's late, and you come on with me and we'll see about them hants."

As there seemed no other way out, the man and woman very reluctantly followed Scotty up to the Ridge. Scotty cooked them all some supper, as is his custom, when he is camping with any one, and they made up their beds and laid down for the night. But all the time the woman was fearful and jumped at every little noise. Scotty said everything was quiet, till along about eleven o'clock when sure enough, he heard some one throwing stones at the rocks. The woman instantly rose right up in bed and called out:

"There, what did I tell you? They're throwing stones at the rocks, this place is haunted. Don't you hear them?"

" Scotty said, sure enough he heard them all right; no doubt about it; and he laid there and tried to figure it out. He'd camped there, off and on, for years and never heard anything like that before. There was no more sleep for any of them. So Scotty took his flash and went walking around the rocks and the noise stopped, though he saw nothing. He went back to bed and the noise started again. He didn't know what to make of it, so he lighted a cigar and laid and waited for morning to dawn. As soon as daylight came, he got up and walked around the rocks and discovered the mystery. He found a coyote that had stuck his head in an empty tomato can some prospector had left, and his nose had caught on the jagged points of tin, in the top where the can had been opened and he couldn't get it off, and at night he had pounded the can around on the rocks, trying to get it off his nose. Scotty caught him, as he was very weak from lack of food, and took the can off and turned him loose. And that ended that particular "hant."

Scotty's life is filled with experiences and he lives them over and over again. He doesn't know what the word "lonely" means. He is absolutely self-sufficient; even when he is a hundred miles from a living soul, which he often is. The only time he even approaches a faint tinge of loneliness, is when he is in town, or when he comes to see us in Chicago and it drizzles. And believe me he doesn't linger long in a place like that. No drizzles for him! He lives a sunny live. Three days is about his limit out in civilization. It's too tame and dreary. The desert is life to him. How could he be lonely there, with the eternal sunshine, great valleys, canyons and mountains to roam and explore! No, he doesn't need society and its drab demands, when he has the vast desert, the glorious sun and his mules. When he starts out with his pack outfit, the world is his. And he prefers to ride mules rather than horses, as they tire less quickly; they can go sixty miles without water. Then too, their feet

32

are smaller and the get over the rocks better and are more sure footed.

Perfume

Scotty is a he man, a he of the he's. And yet he has some very esthetic tastes. He is excessively fond of fine perfumes and indulges this fancy to its limit. Always hidden away, in a dusty grip on the pack mules, or in his car, when he travels, you'll find two or three bottles of the finest perfumes that can be bought. And over and over, when he comes back to the Castle, after having been down to Los Angeles, before he unpacks a thing, he'll pull a dusty old grip out of the car, and out from among the shirts, socks, tooth paste and a conglomerate assortment of plain junk, he'll, triumphantly, produce a choice bottle of Carons, or some other fine perfumer's finest.

"Here Mabel, smell this, it's the world's best, cost twenty five dollars an ounce. Try some." And he'll souse me till I'm reeking with it. But I like it; and so does everybody else.

Often times, when he goes to town, he gets streaks of pulling expensive bottles out of his pockets and tips them up on the lapel of a bellboy's coat or a waiter's cuff.

Not long ago, Al and I went with him into a public garage in Los Angeles, where we had parked our cars. There were two garage men there, dressed in overalls and covered with big black grease spots, and black, greasy hands and faces. Over Scotty goes to his car and pulls out a bottle of "Christmas Night."

"Here," he said, stepping up to the greasy men. "Smell this, it's the world's best, try it." And with that, he tipped the expensive bottle up-side-down on top of the grease and all. The men stood grinning and blushing and one of them said 'I will never dare go home tonight with that on me.' But they liked it.

33

I said to Al, afterwards, "Wasn't that a crime to waste that lovely stuff on those greasy men?"

And he said: "No, these men will always be his friends after this."

And all I could say was: "I guess you are right."

Scotty loves fine cold creams and fancy French soaps, and always has a supply of both in his pack. In the early days, when we first arrived in the Canyon and lived in tents, Scotty would have a nice, clean, wooden dry-goods box set up, for me, in my tent, for a wash stand, a clean towel, a basin and a pitcher of water. Then, a beautiful cake of finely perfumed French soap, that he'd paid a dollar for, and a box of choice powder would be there. Now, you know, you couldn't help but like a man who treats you that way. Then, after we'd wash up, he'd always have a fine dinner, ready to serve, right off the stove, on a box with a paper table cloth over it. Canvas back duck, that he'd shot, on the pond, that morning, a duck apiece with potatoes, preserves, and cake and my! but it tasted good! He is an expert shot. One time, I called to him and told him that two ducks were flying over the camp, and I said:

"O Scotty, I'd love to have them for dinner."

He rushed into the tent, brought out his gun, and watched the ducks, till, in their flight, they came together, and just as they did, he quickly raised his gun, and without apparent aim, never sighted at all, just one shot from the hip, and both ducks fell. He learned to shoot from the hip from Buffalo Bill who was expert at it.

Scotty is a small eater. As a rule, he only eats twice a day, and he breaks all the laws of the health-foodist. He eats, when he feels like it, no regular time, and he eats almost no fruits or green vegetables, never touches salads, and lives on meat, potatoes, white bread, eggs, coffee and lots of desserts and candy; and he is remarkably healthy. But then, you see, he lives in the Desert and breathes the finest air in the world and has no cares or worries. He says there's two things you don't have to worry about, those things you can't help and those things you can. I was worrying the other day, because Al was coming from Chicago in an aeroplane, and there was a storm and the plane was several hours late. He scolded and fussed over my worrying and said:

"Now look here, if he's dead, he's dead that's all, and there aint nothin' to worry about. You got that?" If you can't help it what's the good of worrying.

Soliloquies

Scotty is never more entertaining than after dinner, when we all push our chairs back and he begins. But when we three are alone he always talks much more freely than when others are present.

The other Sunday night, after several carloads of people, from Tonopah, Goldfield and Beatty, had been here and gone, Al and I went to Scotty's room to talk things over. He was lying on the bed, smoking, he nearly always lies down when he smokes, as that bullet, he carries in his right side, pains him if he smokes sitting up.

"Well, Mabel," he said, "How'd you put in the day?"

"Just fine Scotty, how are you?"

"O I'm all right. Now let me tell you something. I aint got much sense and I aint very smart, but nobody's handed it to me yet. Now the trouble with these financiers is, they don't think enough. A lot of them have gone busted because they didn't stop and think. Everybody knows these depressions come in cycles and so on. Now if I was a financier I'd do more thinking. You got that? If they'd do more thinking beforehand, they wouldn't be so sorry afterwards."

"One time I was down on Telescope Peak, on the west side of the Valley. It was about the middle of the afternoon, and all of a sudden I got awful sick. I don't know what was the matter, I don't often get sick, but I'd been up in the snow, the night before, at the top of the Peak; maybe I took cold. Anyway, I felt awful and thought I'd better be getting somewhere and the only place anywheres near was Hungry Bill's camp."

Everybody around the Death Valley country knows about Hungry Bill. He was a powerful big Indian, six feet four and had the reputation of being a tough hombre. He was supposed to have killed several men. For years, Hungry Bill had a camp on the east side of Telescope Peak, about half way up to the mountain, on a ledge; and here he lived, for years, like a regal lord of old. He had fine water, and a small garden spot, and one of the most magnificent views in America from the door of his shack. He could look over the length and breadth of Death Valley, and across the mountains and hundreds of canyons beyond. Here he lived with his very large family, children and grandchildren. He was absolute monarch in his household. He was a heathen and knew nothing of the outside world; the only law he kept was the law of his own will. And all this in the heart of our great civilized America!

And Scotty continued: "So I rode into his camp, and Hungry was there. I told him I was sick and wanted a place to lie down, and I wanted his squaw to wait on me. He grunted and pointed over to the corner of the shack where I could throw my bed. So I got my bed off the mule, and threw it where he told me, and I'm tellin' ya, I was careful to lay with my back close to the wall; I didn't want Hungry to get a chance to get behind me. I wanted to keep him where I could keep my eye on him.

"I happened to have with me a couple of boxes of good cigars, and that night all them Indians was sittin' around, old and young. Two of them oldest boys was as big as Hungry Joe himself, six feet two and four or more. So I took out a cigar and lighted it and I took about three puffs, and here come Hungry's big hand over my face; it looked like a big ham a coming on the end of his long arm. He took the cigar out of my mouth and put it in his own, took about three puffs, and passed it to Mrs. Hungry. She took about three puffs and passed it to the oldest boy, and he took his puffs and passed it to the next. And so that cigar went clear down to the youngest, about fifteen of them altogether; till all the family had a smoke. Then I took out another cigar and lighted it and took three puffs, and sure enough, the same thing happened. This big ham reached over and took it out of my mouth, put it in his own and took three puffs, handed it to his squaw and down the line it went. Well sir, I thought if this is going to keep peace in the family, we'll smoke all night. So that's just what happened; I'd keep a takin them cigars out and lightin them, and Hungry just let me have three puffs that's all, and that's all he took himself, and the family got it. I'll never forget that night, as long as I live, lightin them cigars, and takin three puffs and seein that big ham come over my head.

"Well, Johnson, what you thinking about?"

"I was thinking what a blessing it is, Scott you don't drink any more. When I first knew you, you used to use a funnel; I never saw a man that could take on so much."

"Yes, I used to drink all right, but about ten years ago I got to thinking it over one night, and concluded it wasn't getting me anywhere, and anyway it made me awful sick. I thought I'd live longer if I quit, so I quit, that's all. I ain't took a drop since that night, excepting that night, in the hotel in Hollywood when I was sick, and that doctor put some down me. I ain't seen him since, and if I ever run across him I'll -----" Scotty's language won't bear printing at this point.

"Johnson," and Scotty eyed my husband critically, "Desert clothes don't become you. Why don't you go down to that factory in Los Angeles and get a pair of them landscape pants; you know the kind I mean; they have lines going up and down them and around them, and there's different colors."

"I know what you mean," I said, "You mean checks and plaids."

"Yes, that's it, landscaped all over like the cowboys used to wear when they got dressed up. Johnson always looks good when you see him outside, but he's the toughest looking guy in the Desert. He ought to get some landscape pants." And Scotty went on; "Now you know, Mabel, this publicity stuff, it's all right, but you got to know how to handle it. You always want to remember one thing, it's the galleries that make or break you, it ain't the boxes. I always play to the galleries. Them people in the boxes don't do you no good. They ain't enough of them. But the galleries, they're the ones you want. The firemen, and policemen, shop girls and so on; they're the bunch that make or break you. Always play to the galleries. You got that?"

"Sure Scotty, I got it, it's just a case of majority rules. There's a lot more people in the galleries than in the boxes."

"Now out here in the Desert," he went on to say, "it don't make so much difference, you can play as you want, there aint nobody to take much notice of you. I tell you, Johnson, I've seen them come and I've seen them go. Now look at Rhyolite. There was a time when Rhyolite had ten thousand people in it, and there ain't been nobody there for ten years. It's one of them Nevada ghost towns, nobody lives there but ghosts.

A Chinaman

"I remember coming into Rhyolite one time when she was booming. The gambling joints and dance halls were going full tilt. I'd gone down from the Ranch, on a mule, and I got to drinking and didn't come back home when I was due. I had a Chinaman working for me, at the time, here in the canyon, and when I didn't show up on time, he got on a horse and came to Rhyolite after me. Now there was a bunch of roughnecks running Rhyolite, and they said no Chinaman could eat there or stay there over night, and that my Chink would have to get out of town right away. They had the boarding houses all scared and they wouldn't give him anything to eat. Well, I said, that Chinaman's got to eat; so I went up to the Prosecuting Attorney's office and told him the situation. He agreed with me and he said a man had to eat even if he was a Chinaman. So he told me to go ahead and handle it the best I could, and he'd stand by me. So I took the Chinaman to a boarding house and told the proprietor I wanted dinner, and I had my man with me, and he'd eat with me and that he was a Chinaman. The proprietor said, no, he couldn't feed the Chinaman, but he'd feed me. I said: 'to hell with you, that Chinaman's going to eat.' So I went back to see the Prosecuting Attorney and told Sometimes I think he is too kind. He picks up all the stray mongrels he meets and brings them home and tells John to the window, of his office, with his gun, and if anything happened to stand by me. He said he would. So I went out and bought a lot of dinner, and got it on plates, and I took the Chinaman, and we went out in the middle of the street and sat down, and I had my gun across my knee, in case there was any commotion. And we ate dinner; and the Prosecuting Attorney sat in his office, with his gun, watching us out the window. I had another man watching out another window, with a

39

Scotty and Chinaman - circa 1907

gun too; but no trouble started, and the Chinaman and I ate all right. A man has to eat even if he is a Chink.

"Well, I didn't want to go out of town that night, it was too late, so after eating in the middle of the main street of Rhyolite, I didn't have no trouble getting a place for the Chinaman to sleep. The Chinaman and I stayed all night and rode back to the ranch the next morning."

Dogs

Whatever may be Scotty's faults, he has a tender heart underneath, and he will never stand for injustice around him. I have spoken before of his kindness to animals, especially dogs. Sometimes I think he is too kind. He picks up all the stray mongrels he meets and brings them home and tells John to feed them, and the result is, the canyon is full of curs. I counted six of them running around outside the Castle today. But they are all thoroughbreds, and the finest kind of dogs, to Scotty. He'll tell you the fine points of every one of them. I said to him only yesterday, "Scotty, why don't you get rid of all of these mongrels and get one good police dog?"

"What's the matter with them dogs," he said, "Them's good dogs, they're all good barkers."

"Yes, they're good barkers all right, they bark at anything. Now a good police dog would only bark when there was something to bark about; but this bunch bark at the moon if there isn't anything else to bark at."

"That's what we want," he said, "plenty of bark."

Moonlight

There are many beautiful scenes in this world. Moonlight on the ocean has it charm. Moonlight anywhere is a delight. But there's no moonlight in the world that can compare with the moonlight in Grapevine Canyon, our desert canyon, where the Castle stands. Last night the moon was at its full, and we went out on the upper porch and looked down the Canyon and across Death Valley. There are some things one cannot put into words, emotions, that surge through the heart; scenes, that fill us, and thrill us, and woo us; such was the scene that we looked upon last night. Something about the clear desert atmosphere seems to make the moonlight brighter than anywhere else in the world, and to glorify it. And the great mountains rise in the splendor of it all. Moonlight in the Desert! You may have your cities and electric lights, movies, dancing parties, and surging crowds; but, for a thrill, an emotion, a sense of peace, and a confidence in a God who cares, give me moonlight in the Desert.

Irene Watkins

One of the interesting things in Scotty's character is his memory of details, especially of instances in his early life. He was narrating, not long ago, in one of his after dinner talks at the Castle, a little affair that took place in New York City years ago.

In his own words: "I'd gone there to enter the Wild West Show and was a little early for the opening. There was a "Dog and Cat" show going on at Madison Square Garden, and a man I knew, who ran a small newspaper, told me about it and said it wasn't doing very well, nobody much was coming. So I thought, as I hadn't anything much to do while I was waiting there, I'd see what I could do to help put that dog and cat show on the map. I went down and saw the newspaper man, and got him interested, and we went down to the saloon, where I'd seen a cat hanging around in the alley. It belonged to the saloon. I paid them a dollar for it, and it was a right good-looking cat for an alley cat.

"I knew the manicure girl at the Hoffman House, so I took the cat to her and got her to fix it up. She manicured the cat's nails and put pink color on them, then she washed its fur with Chinese shavings, and that made it stand all out and kind of curl; and when she got through with it, it was a good-looking cat, I'm telling ya.

"We named the cat 'Irene Watkins.' Then I went to a concern that made fine cages and they give me one of their best cages for Irene Watkins, for the cat show. The Wild West Show hadn't begun yet, so I got one of the 'peanuts and popcorn' boys with the Wild West Show, who was waiting just like I was, to be an attendant for Irene. One of the best clothing houses in New York give him a uniform, with fancy gold braid on it, and 'Irene Watkins,' in gold letters on the collar. He stood beside Irene's cage in the show. In the meantime, the newspaper man was feeding this stuff every day to the newspapers, and all these concerns were glad to furnish their stuff for the publicity they were getting. Then, I arranged with a high class restaurant across the street, to have a special waiter bring Irene's meals over to the show regularly, on a silver tray, in one of them silver dishes with a cover on top of it to keep it warm. He'd come across the street, bouncing the silver tray over his shoulder, several times a day. In the dish was fish fins. Irene Watkins would paw them over but never deign to eat them. You see we always give her liver and cream, nights, after the crowd was gone. Then I got a jeweler, on Fifth Avenue, to make a bracelet, all covered with diamonds, for Irene's front left paw, and on her right paw we put a big diamond solitaire. Then we rubbed catnip on the bottom of her right foot, and there she'd sit with her left foot down with this wide band of diamonds on it, and she'd be licking her right foot, flashing that big solitaire.

"In the meantime the newspaper man was getting out extras regarding Irene Watkins. Well, say! Did the crowds come? Well I should say they did come. That show went on the map. They had to have a special policeman stand by Irene's cage to watch them diamond bracelets and handle the crowd. The manicure girl came over every day and manicured Irene's nails right before the crowd. You never could get near the cage when she was there. At the end of the show, the judges give Irene Watkins first prize and gave me $20.00 but the paper came out the next day and said I wasn't going to keep the money because the judges was under a false impression. You see, Irene Watkins was a tom-cat and they didn't know it. I sold Irene for $200.00 and give the money to the Children's Hospital and the Dog and Cat Show moved out and the Wild West show moved in.

Callers

"Well," he said, "living in this world ain't so bad if you don't worry, just take things as they are. Now I've lived in this Canyon a long while, and I've seen them come and I've seen them go.

"I remember one time when we was livin' in the tents; we used to have the drinking water in a five gallon bottle, all wrapped in gunney sacks. We hung it up in the willow tree, about a hundred feet from the tents. It was hung in a rope sling and kind of balanced, so when you wanted a drink you could tip it, easy; then, after you drank, you always took a little water and wet the gunney sacks around it to keep it wet, and that kept the water cool.

"One afternoon a man and woman and their daughter, she must a been about nineteen years old, drove in. They was going down into the Valley. It was too late to go any further that night, so I give them your tent, Johnson. Well, that evening we was all standing down under the willow, and I was showing them how to get a drink, and the mules was hanging around, and the woman, she patted Mose's face, (Mose is Scotty's special mule) and she struck one of them attitudes, and she said: "Mules are some of God's noblest creatures'. I didn't say nothin, but I thought I'd seen some of God's noblest creatures do some pretty devilish actin. Well, we all went to bed, and along about two in the morning, Daughter wanted a drink, so she got up and started for the water bottle in the willow tree. Now it was dark and she didn't know that the mules always slept under the willow tree, and laid around there. So, just as she got to the tree, she fell over a mule, he rose right up and threw her over on another mule, and that mule threw her again, and O, the world was full of mules. I'm tellin ya. She finally landed on Mose and held on to him and he started down the canyon to the fence and threw her over in-to the field. By this time, Mother had missed Daughter, and she got up Father and they began to call, and the mules were all a champin and a brayin and all Hell was loose. So I got up and got into my trousers, and lighted the lantern, and started out. We found Daughter down in the field, where Mose had thrown her. We picked her up and brought her up and laid her out on a table. I thought it might be curtains for her, but she didn't have any bones broke and wasn't so much hurt after all, just shook up some. The next morning they went down the Canyon, but they never said another word about them mules being God's noblest creatures."

A Tragedy

"A great deal has been said and written about the heat of Death Valley. Much of what we hear is true for four months of the year, from the middle of May to the middle of September. But people don't realize that for the rest of the year, the days are, for the most part, perfect and the nights cold. Indeed, during the winter, many a time I have needed a fur coat, quite as much as in Chicago. Our own Canyon is three thousand feet high, and during the winter, we need heat night and morning and often all day.

The intense heat of the summer is not all to the bad, however. There's some good in most everything in this world, if we look for it. The heat in Death Valley in summer, if handled in the right way, is marvelous for nose, throat and sinus infections. A wealthy man, in New York City, had been operated on five times in New York and Washington for sinus infection, and when the doctors ordered another operation, he rebelled and said he was going to try Death Valley in July. He came to Los Angeles and bought him a small car, and made for the desert. He arranged for a place to sleep high up where it would be cool at night, then each day he drove down into a temperature of one hundred and twenty degrees in the shade; he found a shady place to read and eat his lunch, and spent a good bit of time right out in the hot sun. In two weeks he went back to New York, well enough to enjoy the winter at home. For several summers he has done this, and finds that his trouble has disappeared.

Another friend, who coughed constantly all winter, following pneumonia, came to visit us and her cough left in an hour after arriving here and never returned. The heat is also good for some forms of kidney trouble. But, while a little of the Desert heat, is good for some conditions, too much of it is not so good, and it should be taken with widsom and knowledge like any other treatment. Even good things can be over done.

Others have written of the death of James Dayton, in the heat of Death Valley; but perhaps you would like to hear Scotty's version of it.

"You see it was this way; down in Death Valley sink, bout

three hundred feet below sea level, is Furnace Creek Ranch. It belongs to the Borax people. It's awful hot there in summer, often a hundred and thirty and thirty-five in the shade. They had a man staying there one summer, by the name of Dayton. He was super on the Ranch. In the middle of July, when the heat was at its worst, he concluded to drive out to Barstow. He started one morning with a wagon and team across the Sink. They's sent out word he was coming; so when he failed to show up in reasonable time, they got back word to the Ranch, and they went out to look for him. He'd been gone a week. They'd gone about thirty miles when they saw his dog running around in the mesquite and that gave them a clue. They went over to where the dog was, and there was the wagon, and the horses, still hitched to it, dead. They had struggled to get loose from the harness but hadn't quite made it; if they had given one more struggle, they'd been loose. There was a cat in the box on the wagon, and it was dead. There was a whole barrel of water on the wagon; so he didn't get out of water, he must have gotten overcome with the terrible heat; for there he sat, over under a grease-wood bush, with his head hanging over his knees, dead. Well, there wasn't anything to do but bury him. So they dug a grave right there, where he died, and they wrapped him up in some canvas they had, and as they dropped him in, one of the men give him a funeral. He said: 'You've lived in heat, you've died in heat, and now you've gone to Hell.' They buried him in Death Valley, near Furnace Creek, at the foot of the Funeral Mountains. Then, later, the bones of the horses were scattered over the top of the grave, and they're there today, bleached out by the sun."

That was a heat tragedy, but just a few days ago, a cold-tragedy occurred a few miles north of us. A cold blizzard gripped the ranges round about. Three men started out in their car, on a well-traveled road, for Goldfield, about forty miles

47

away. They had gone about twenty miles when their car broke down.

Now, if this had happened to Scotty, it would not have been so serious; for Scotty is heat wise, cold wise, and desert wise generally. He is always prepared for all emergencies. He would have stayed right with his car, and would have had plenty of food, water and warm blankets, and, at this time of year, a down-filled canvas. Cold would have been a small matter to him. He drives an air-cooled car; so his radiator wouldn't have frozen. He would have wrapped himself up in his downey bed and blankets, after a good meal, and quietly waited, smoked or slept till the storm was over; maybe a week. Time means nothing to him when the elements are not favorable. Then, he would have drawn the oil off his car, in a five gallon can, sliced some bacon and lighted it, made a little fire with some of the oil and the bacon, heated the oil and poured the warm oil back in the engine; so it would have started quickly, and he would have gone serenely on his way.

But two of these three men were not old timers. They were young men, between twenty and thirty years old and the other man was middle-aged. They did the most foolish thing they could do. They started to walk to Goldfield, twenty miles away, in the midst of a snow storm and high wind. When they had walked for hours and had gone fifteen miles, the two young men gave out, and refused to go farther. So they spent the night, right where they were. They built a shelter of snow and laid close together to keep warm. But the feet of the two young men froze; so the older man pushed on alone, in the morning through the snow, and said he'd send help back to them. It took him several hours to walk five miles. He staggered into Goldfield exhausted. He told of the two men left behind and Mr. Edward Giles and Geo. Vidovich of Goldfield, immediately started out, with hot coffee and food to rescue the men, but were unable to find them. Later, another party went out and found them, dead.

This all happened within fifty miles of the Castle. Goldfield is six thousand feet high while the Castle is three thousand feet high and is nestled away in a small protected canyon. Storms may be raging all around, but there's 'peace in the nest' and we are warm and safe and cozy, as the country round about is trapped in the arms of a raging blizzard and the mountains are blanketed in snow. Those who live in the Death Valley Country realize that it is not to be trifled with, either in summer or winter. It is a stern country and merciless to the unwise stranger, but protective and full of alluring interest to old timers.

While travelling the desert today with all the conveniences and improvements of modern travel, such as oil roads, water barrels along the side of the highway; patrols, frequent filling stations, hotels and camps with every comfort, one can hardly conceive the hardships, the hazards, the loneliness, the isolation and the danger of travel in the desert mountain country in the days of the pioneer.

While the danger and the hazards have gone, there still is probably no portion of the desert and mountain country where one can better recapture the atmosphere and feeling of the old frontier and pioneer days, while still travelling in safety and comfort, than in Death Valley today. Many are now travelling through the Valley today both in summer and winter.

Life and death

For nearly thirty years, Scotty, Al and I, have travelled the dreary wastes of Death Valley. In heat that was unbearable, in cold that froze you to the marrow, in sand storms that blinded and cut; down, down, in Death Valley where the hot winds blow!

We never could have stood it all these years, had it not been for the mountains of Life, round about. All around Death Valley are great mountain ranges. When we couldn't bear it in the Valley for the heat, we would always make for the mountains. There it was cool and refreshing, and there was protection, water and food. Wonderful mountain sheep, quail, berries, pinion nuts and refreshing springs of water.

We are all living in Death Valley, in this world. This is a dying world. The doctor's offices are full; the hospitals, and operating rooms, are crowded. There are drug stores, on every corner with their pills and powders, and there are sanitariums and health-food shops: but round about this old dying world are God's mountain ranges of Life, with their peaks of mercy, love, kindness and justice.

Just across the Valley from Furnace Creek, stands the highest peak in the Death Valley Country, Telescope Peak. You can climb to the top of this great mountain and look down into the lowest point in the United States, nearly 300 ft. below sea level, and by just turning your head, you can look up to the highest point in this country, Mount Whitney, nearly 15,000 ft. high - from the lowest to the highest!

There are times when you can stand on top of Telescope Peak and look down into a temperature of 130° in the shade and up to snow on Mount Whitney.

In God's mountain ranges of life and hope round about this dying world, there is also an outstanding peak, Mount Calvary! And you can stand on Calvary's Heights today and look down into the lowest depths of Hell and by turning your eyes you can look up into the heights of Glory — and it isn't very far from the depths of Death Valley to the heights of Mt. Whitney, only Telescope Peak stands between — and it isn't very far from the depths of Hell to the heights of Glory, only Calvary stands between!

51